How to Train Your
Siberian Husky

liz palika

SIBERIAN HUSKY

Photos by the author unless
otherwise credited.

The Publisher would like to thank handler Jennifer Grosiak for participating
in the training photos for this book.

Distributed in the UNITED STATES to the Pet Trade by T.F.H. Publications,
Inc., One T.F.H. Plaza, Neptune City, NJ 07753; on the Internet at
www.tfh.com; in CANADA Rolf C. Hagen Inc., 3225 Sartelon St. Laurent-
Montreal Quebec H4R 1E8; Pet Trade by H & L Pet Supplies Inc., 27 Kingston
Crescent, Kitchener, Ontario N2B 2T6; in ENGLAND by T.F.H. Publications,
PO Box 15, Waterlooville PO7 6BQ; in AUSTRALIA AND THE SOUTH PACIFIC
by T.F.H. (Australia), Pty. Ltd., Box 149, Brookvale 2100 N.S.W., Australia; in
NEW ZEALAND by Brooklands Aquarium Ltd. 5 McGiven Drive, New Ply-
mouth, RD1 New Zealand; in SOUTH AFRICA, Rolf C. Hagen S.A. (PTY.) LTD.
P.O. Box 201199, Durban North 4016, South Africa; in Japan by T.F.H.
Publications, Japan—Jiro Tsuda, 10-12-3 Ohjidai, Sakura, Chiba 285, Japan.
Published by T.F.H. Publications, Inc.
MANUFACTURED IN THE UNITED STATES OF AMERICA
BY T.F.H. PUBLICATIONS, INC.

contents

Introduction **4**

1 Selecting the Right Dog for You **6**

2 Canine Development Stages **19**

3 All About Formal Training **30**

4 Early Puppy Training **38**

5 The Basic Obedience Commands **50**

6 Advanced Training and Dog Sports **64**

7 Problem Prevention and Solving **76**

8 Have Some Fun With Your Training! **86**

Suggested Reading **94**

INTRODUCTION

Photo by Isabelle Francais.

The Siberian Husky's high degree of intelligence makes him an ideal student for training.

breed, and Huskies are no exception. Now, don't get me wrong, Siberian Huskies are nice dogs! However, they are not the right dog for everyone. Prospective dog owners need to understand the breed they are considering—whether it is a Cocker, Lab, Siberian, or Doberman Pinscher.

Prospective owners also need to know that there are other options than simply buying a puppy. Puppies are a lot of work and take a long time

Double take! When selecting your pup, don't worry if you can't choose one—two will do very well together.

I have been teaching dog obedience classes for over 20 years and see, on the average, more than a thousand dogs and owners per year. Through the years I have seen a number of different breeds rise and fall in popularity. For a few years German Shepherds were the rage, Poodles came and went, then Labrador Retrievers. Today, Siberian Huskies are the breed of choice for many people.

As an obedience instructor, I always have misgivings when people buy the "popular"

Photo by Isabelle Francais.

to grow up. Adopting an older puppy, a young adult, or even a mature dog might be a better choice for many people.

In this book I have tried to present Siberian Husky owners (and prospective Husky owners) with choices about choosing a dog and good effective information on how to make that dog a well-behaved member of the family. Siberian Huskies can be fun-loving, energetic clowns, as well as sensitive, intelligent, serious, hard-working dogs. With training and help from their owner, they can be a friend, a partner, and a great companion.

Like all dogs, Siberian Huskies are pack animals and enjoy each other's company.

A Husky makes a great pet for children because he is tolerant and often very affectionate.

siberian husky

SELECTING
the Right Dog for You

WHAT ARE SIBERIAN HUSKIES?

Siberian Huskies are an ancient breed, with a known history dating back thousands of years. Originally bred as sled dogs, these beautiful but very hard-working dogs were hooked to sleds in teams of six or more and were capable of pulling heavy loads great distances. Today, Siberians are very much a part of modern life and are wonderful companion dogs. An active breed, Siberians love to camp and hike, walk, jog, pull sleds and wagons, and play with the family's children.

Temperament

Siberian Huskies are fun-loving dogs. Very people oriented, Siberians need to spend time with their people; time to play, exercise, learn obedience skills and social rules, and even just quiet time. This desire to be with people affects

This dog has the keen, alert expression characteristic of the Siberian Husky. By nature, Siberians are active dogs and will need acceptable outlets, such as safe toys, for their energy.

siberian husky

all aspects of his life. A Siberian is not a good dog to be left alone in the backyard all day. When bored and lonely, the Siberian may become destructive, digging up the yard, ripping up your garden, or tearing up the garden furniture. In a desire to be with people, some Siberians become incredible escape artists—jumping over fences or digging out of the yard.

given any excuse to do so. If you decide to add a Siberian Husky to your life, you better like to laugh!

Physical Appearance

Siberian Huskies are medium-sized dogs, no taller than 23 inches at the shoulder, and between 35 to 60 pounds in weight. The bitches are smaller and more feminine in

Although all colors from black to pure white are acceptable in the standard, this beautiful mother and child show off their black, white, and gray markings.

Siberians can find the fun in anything and will. Puppies will play with anything and love chasing butterflies, balls, toys, and even airplanes high in the sky. Even grown-up mature adults retain a sense of fun and will turn into a clown when

appearance. The Siberian has the dense coat, brush tail, and erect ears normally associated with the northern breeds. The Siberian Husky is a working breed and should appear athletic and able to do the work for which it was bred.

Photo by Isabelle Francais.

Siberians are very energetic puppies and require sufficient time outside to play.

IS A SIBERIAN THE RIGHT DOG FOR YOU?

Evaluating Your Personality and Lifestyle

The decision to add a dog to your family is not a decision that should be taken lightly. This is a 14- to 15-year commitment and although Siberian Huskies are, for the most part, easy-going dogs, they are active, free-spirited, and do have some specific needs.

Do you work long hours, and are you tired and just want to relax when you come home, preferring to spend the evening reading or watching television? If this is you, a calm older Siberian might be good for you. Do you come home tired but like to get outside, walking or riding your bicycle? If so, a calm adult dog might suit your needs. Do you work at home, have short work hours, and enjoy doing things? If so, a puppy or an active young dog should please you.

Being the center of a dog's world can be thrilling to some people and overwhelming to others. If you don't like being followed or watched, don't get a Siberian Husky. A Siberian will want to follow you from room to room and will be heartbroken even if you go to the bathroom without him. When you sit down, the Siberian will want to lie down nearby. When you leave the house, the Siberian will want to go with you. Obviously, having a dog with you 24 hours a day is impossible for most people; however, if you own a Siberian Husky, you will need to be able to provide him with as much companionship as possible.

What is your life like? Are you retired and live alone? If you are and your health is good, either a puppy or an adult

As Siberians grow older, they settle down and become better suited to the lifestyle of a retiree or very busy adult.

Photo by Isabelle Francais.

Siberian might be good dog for you. Are there active children in the house? Siberians can be wonderful with children as long as there is adult supervision and the dog is taught good social rules. However, if you work full time and live alone, a Siberian might not be the best choice—as was mentioned earlier, a Siberian alone is a lonely unhappy dog.

The Dog's Needs

Before you decide to add a Siberian Husky to your family, make sure you can fulfill the dog's needs. First of all, your time and companionship is of the utmost importance. As was mentioned earlier, Siberians do very poorly alone in a backyard all day. This is a companion breed that needs to spend time with you.

You will also have to have a securely fenced yard. As a working dog, Siberians are very curious and given a chance, will wander off to explore. A large yard is wonderful, but even a dog run (no smaller than 10 feet by 30 feet) is acceptable as long as the dog gets plenty of time out of the run with you.

You must also have some means of exercising the dog. If you like to go jogging, that's fine, but if you are not a jogger, you will need to think of an alternative. Perhaps you can teach the dog to run next to your bicycle or you can take the dog swimming on a regular basis. A young healthy Siberian should NOT be a couch potato!

SELECTING THE RIGHT DOG

Male or Female?

There are a lot of myths concerning the personality traits of both males and females. Ultimately it depends upon the personality of the individual dog. Spayed or neutered bitches and dogs are usually a little calmer than those that are not; spaying and neutering removes the sexual hormones and, as a result, the sexual tension that can accompany those hormones. To be a good pet and companion, your Siberian doesn't need those hormones anyway.

What Age?

Puppies are adorable, especially Siberian puppies. When you add a puppy to your family, it is just like adding a baby to your family. In fact, in many ways, raising a puppy is much like raising a child except that the puppy will grow up faster. As the puppy learns and

grows, he will become an integral part of your family, and by the time your puppy has grown up (two years or so), your young Siberian Husky will have become a good friend.

MONEY MATTERS

Do you have the financial means to care for this dog? Good quality food is not inexpensive, nor is veterinary care. Your dog will need vaccinations, regular checkups, and will need to be spayed or neutered. You will need grooming supplies, including brushes, nail clippers, and flea and tick control products. If you do not know how to thoroughly groom your dog, you will need to pay for regular visits (every six weeks or so) to the grooming salon. Your dog will need a collar, a leash or two, and a kennel crate. You will also need to invest in an obedience class (or two!). At some point during the dog's lifetime, there may be an emergency veterinary call because of an injury or illness. You will need the financial resources to care for your dog and must never delay needed care because of a lack of money.

However, it takes a lot of work to raise a puppy and for many people, adding a puppy to their life might not be the best choice. But that doesn't

Photo by Isabelle Francais.

These little rascals are hard to resist, but make sure your decision to purchase a puppy is well thought out.

mean those people cannot have a dog. There are many adult Siberian Huskies that need homes and these dogs could be just the answer for people who do not have the time to spend with a young puppy. With an adult dog, you know what you're getting. You know how big the dog is, what the adult personality is like, and the state of the dog's health. With a puppy, some of these things are unknown until the puppy grows up.

There are, of course, some negative factors about adopting an adult dog. Adopting an adult is sometimes like buying a used car—you don't know how it has been treated prior to your ownership and that can affect future behavior. Many times the adult dog's past health history is unknown. Newly adopted adult dogs also must have time to settle into their new homes. Time must be allowed for emotional and physical adjustment.

Finding an Adult Dog

If you have decided that an adult Siberian would be better for you, there are many places that may have the right dog for you. Many Siberians are given up by their owners for a variety of reasons. Some people didn't research the breed and found

siberian husky

after a few months that a Siberian was not the right breed for them. Other people may not have been willing to give their Siberian the time and training the dog needed. Or perhaps there was an emergency, for example, the owner may have passed away and family members were unable to keep the dog. Check for these dogs at your local humane society or shelter.

Evaluating an Adult Dog

Once you have found an adult Siberian Husky that you like, how do you decide if he is the right dog for you? Well,

emotions certainly play a part—do you like this dog? There is more of a chance of success in this new relationship if you and the dog like each other. However, there should be more to the decision-making process than just emotions.

Do you know why the dog was given up by his original owners? Sometimes the dog is given up through no fault of his own—maybe his owner was transferred overseas or his owner passed away. However, if the owner gave the dog up because of behavior problems, you need to know that. Has the dog had any obedience training? Is the dog housetrained?

This dog's happy expression and willingness to make eye contact indicate a friendly disposition.

Photo by Isabelle Francais.

Many beautiful, well-adjusted dogs, like this stunning Siberian, are available at your local shelter.

These are important issues, because even if you are willing to do some training with the dog, housetraining a previously untrained adult Siberian can be a tremendous task!

What is the dog's personality like? When you whistle or speak to the dog, does he look at you happily, wagging his bushy tail? If he does, that is great. If he looks sideways at you, slinks away, or bares his throat, be careful. He could be afraid or worried because of previous mistreatment. An unknown fearful dog might also bite. Be careful, too, if the dog stares at

RESCUE GROUPS

Many breed clubs also sponsor or run breed rescue groups. Rescue groups screen the dogs they take in for adoption. Dogs are checked for personality or temperament flaws (such as aggression) and their obedience skills (or lack thereof) are evaluated. The dogs are vaccinated, and, if needed, spayed or neutered. This screening process can be invaluable to you, the potential adopter. To find a Siberian rescue group in your area, call the American Siberian Huskies rescue coordinator.

Photo by Isabelle Francais.

Siberian Huskies were bred to work outdoors and always enjoy a romp in the crisp fall air.

you, making eye contact without wagging his tail. This could be a potentially aggressive dog.

Ideally, you want a dog that is happy to see you without showing too much worry or fear and without showing any aggression. You want a dog that is housetrained and who has had some obedience training. Make sure that the dog's behavior problems are ones that you can live with for the time being and are willing to work on in the future.

Ideally, too, the dog has already been spayed or neutered, is vaccinated, and is healthy.

Finding a Puppy

If you have the time, resources, and patience to raise a puppy, you will want to find a reputable breeder. Breeder referrals can come from many sources. People walking their dog might refer you to their breeder. A veterinarian, groomer, or trainer may know of some reputable breeders. Many of the national dog magazines have classified ad sections where breeders can advertise. You might also want to attend a dog show in your community and talk to the people attending the show.

Once you find a few breeders, ask for an appointment to

meet with them. At your meeting, ask the breeders a few questions. "Are you active in the dog world?" This answer will tell you many things. First, if the breeders show their dogs in conformation competition, be up-to-date on news about the breed. Breed club newsletters and magazines usually publish health-related issues, including genetic or inherited problems and potential treatments.

Although some traits are inherited within a breed, every Siberian Husky is an individual with his own personality.

their dogs are probably good examples of the breed. If they show in obedience competition, their dogs are trainable. If they show their dogs in sledding or carting trials, their dogs have the working instincts Siberians are supposed to have.

"Do you belong to the Siberian Husky Club of America, as well as local or regional clubs?" If the breeder does, they are more likely to

"What health problems have you seen in your dogs?" If the breeder says none, be skeptical. Even though Huskies are normally healthy dogs, a breed or line with absolutely no health problems is rare. Siberian Huskies can have a number of health problems including epilepsy, cataracts, and other disorders such as allergies. Reputable breeders should be honest with you about potential health problems and what they are doing to try to prevent future problems.

"Can you provide me with a list of references?" Keep in mind that this list will consist of people the breeder knows are happy with his dogs, but it can still serve a purpose. You can

of their puppies. Don't get defensive; they are trying to do the right thing. Instead, answer the questions honestly. If by some chance, a particular breeder says that her dogs are not right for you, listen to her— she knows her dogs better than you do.

Photo by Isabelle Francais.

Socialization with littermates is very important for a well-adjusted Husky. These playful, active pups are the pictures of health.

still ask them about their experience. "Did the breeder work well with them? Would they buy from the breeder again?"

Caring breeders will ask you as many questions as you ask them. They want to know if you are the right person to buy one

Evaluating a Puppy

Each puppy has his own personality and finding the right personality to match yours is sometimes a challenge. For example, if you are outgoing, extroverted, and active, a quiet, withdrawn, submissive puppy would not fit well into your household and lifestyle. You will need a puppy more like you. However, that quiet puppy might do very well for a quiet person or a less active retiree.

When you go to look at a puppy or a litter of puppies, there are a few things you can do with the puppy to help evaluate the puppy's personality. First, with the puppy away from his mother and littermates, place the puppy on the ground and walk a few steps away. Squat down and call the puppy to you. An outgoing extroverted Siberian puppy will come happily and try to climb into your lap. If you stand up and walk away, the extrovert will follow you, trying to get under foot. If you crumple up a piece of paper and throw it six feet away, he will dash after it and bring it back proudly. This Siberian would do well with an owner who is just as much an extrovert as he is. He will need training, lots of exercise, and a job to occupy his mind.

A quiet submissive puppy will come to you when you call but may do a belly crawl, or may roll over and bare her belly. When you get up to walk away, the submissive puppy may watch you but may be hesitant to follow you. If you

toss the piece of paper for her, she may go after it and bring it part way back, but may be hesitant to bring it directly to you. This puppy will need a quiet owner, gentle handling, and positive training to build her confidence.

These two puppies are the extremes; most Siberians are somewhere in between these two personality types. Try to find a puppy that will be comfortable with your personality, your family, and your lifestyle. Don't get a pushy dominant puppy and hope to change him; he may learn control with training but he will always have that personality. Nor should you get the quiet submissive puppy because you feel sorry for her. Find the puppy that is right for you.

An extroverted puppy will come to you eagerly and greet you with confidence.

Photo by Isabelle Francais.

BE CAREFUL!

Adding a dog to your family should be a time of anticipation and excitement, but it also requires thought, research, and preparation to prevent the experience from becoming a nightmare. Unfortunately, horror stories abound of purebred dogs plagued with health problems, or breeders who misrepresented their dogs or who didn't come through with the promised paperwork. Hopefully, this Siberian Husky will be a part of your life for the next 12 to 14 years, so make sure a Siberian is the right dog for you and choose carefully.

Reputable breeders will only use the best quality dogs in order to produce healthy puppies.

Photo by Isabelle Francais.

The Siberian Husky you choose should be bright-eyed, healthy, and interested in the world around him.

Photo by Isabelle Francais.

siberian husky

Canine
DEVELOPMENT
Stages

IN THE BEGINNING

Even though dogs and people have lived together for thousands of years, the bond that we have with dogs when and how the bond develops, it is important to understand that a dog is a unique creature, not a person in a fuzzy dog suit.

The ancient origins of our beloved dogs are readily apparent in the wolf-like features of the Siberian Husky.

Photo by Isabelle Francais.

must be renewed with each puppy. The bond itself is not hereditary, although the tendency and ability to bond are. This relationship between a dog and owner is what makes owning a dog so special, but it doesn't happen automatically. To understand

FAMILIES AND PACKS

Most researchers agree that thousands of years ago the first domesticated dogs were descended from wolves. Wolves are very social creatures and live in an extended family pack. The pack might consist of a dominant male and a dominant female (usually the only ones who breed) as well as a few subordinate adults, juveniles, and puppies. This a very harmonious group who hunt together, play together, defend their territory against intruders, and care for each other and the pack's young. The only discord happens when there is a change in the pack order. If an adult of some status dies or leaves the pack, or if a youngster tries to assume dominance, there might be some jockeying around to fill that position.

Many experts feel that domestic dogs adapt so well to our lifestyle because we also live in groups, although our groups are called families instead of packs. However, the comparison really isn't accurate—our families are much more chaotic than the average wolf pack! We are terribly inconsistent with our social rules and rules for behavior. (We let the dog up on the couch when he's clean but yell at him when he jumps up with muddy paws!) To the dog, our communication skills are confusing. Our voices say one thing while our body language says another. To our dogs, people are very complex confusing creatures. So yes, we can say that both dogs and

Photo by Isabelle Francais.

During the first weeks of life, a Siberian puppy depends on his mother to fulfill all his needs.

humans live in social groups and we can use that comparison to understand a little more about our dogs. However, we must also understand that our families are very different from a wolf pack.

FROM BIRTH TO FOUR WEEKS OF AGE

For the first three weeks of life, the family and the pack are unimportant as far as the baby Siberian Husky is concerned. The only one of any significance is his mother. She is the key to his survival and is the source of food, warmth, and security.

At four weeks of age, the baby Siberian's needs are still centered on his mother, but his littermates are becoming more important. Littermates provide warmth and security when mom leaves the nest. During this period he will learn to use his senses to follow sounds and to focus his eyes. His curiosity about the world around him is developing and he will start exploring his nest or whelping box.

Mom will also start disciplining the puppies now, and her instinctive training is vitally important to the puppies' future acceptance of discipline and training. We can also learn a lot by watching mom discipline her babies.

The breeder should be handling the puppies during this period, gentling touching and massaging them. The puppies will learn the difference between their mom's caresses and those from people.

WEEKS FIVE THROUGH SEVEN

The baby Siberian goes through some tremendous changes between five and seven weeks of age. He is learning to recognize people and is starting

This cuddly Siberian Husky pup settles down for a nap with his littermates, who are an important source of warmth and security.

Photo by Isabelle Francais.

to respond to individual voices. He is playing more with his littermates and the wrestling and scuffling teaches each puppy how to get along, how to play, when the play is too rough, when to be submissive, and what to take seriously. Mom's discipline at this point teaches the puppy to accept discipline, correction, training, and affection.

MOTHER LOVE

Gracie is a dark gray Siberian Husky, an American Kennel Club conformation champion, an obedience champion, a Companion Dog, and an experienced sled dog. She is also a very good mother. When one of her puppies bites too hard, her correction is short, sharp, fair and firm: a growl and a muzzle bite that ceases as soon as the puppy reacts submissively. Every correction is followed by love and affection and she never holds a grudge.

This is a good time for the puppy to meet other people. The breeder should supervise all visits so that the puppy isn't handled too roughly or frightened, of course, but friendly handling and play will help socialize the puppy to people.

If the puppy is taken from his mother and littermates during this time frame, he may have lasting behavioral problems. He may have difficulty dealing with other dogs, have problems accepting rules and discipline, and may turn excessively shy or excessively aggressive because of fear.

THE EIGHTH WEEK

The eighth week of life is a frightening time for most puppies. Puppies go through several fear periods and this is the first one. Even though this is the traditional time for most puppies to go to their new homes, they would actually benefit tremendously by staying with their mom and

Exploring the great outdoors is an important part of the socialization process. New experiences will enrich his life and make him an active participant in his own socialization.

Photo by Isabelle Francais.

Photo by Isabelle Francais.

Wrestling and play fighting is a natural part of puppy life that teaches young Siberian Huskies how to interact with other dogs.

littermates for one more week. If the puppy leaves his breeder's home during the eighth week of life and is frightened by the car ride to his new home, he may retain that fear of car rides for the rest of his life. The same applies to his new home, the new sounds in the house, the trip to the veterinarian's office, or anything else that frightens him.

WEEKS NINE TO TWELVE

The baby Siberian can go to his new home anytime during the ninth and tenth weeks of life. At this age, he is ready to form permanent relationships. Take advantage of this and spend time with your new puppy, playing with him, cuddling with him, and encouraging him to explore his new world. Teach him his name by calling him a high-pitched tone of voice, especially when he is already moving towards you. (Never use his name to scold him!) Encourage the puppy to follow you by backing away from him, patting your leg, or clapping your hands.

Socialization is very important now. Socialization is more than simply introducing your puppy to other people, dogs, noises, and sounds. It is making sure that your baby Siberian is not frightened by these things and that he is introduced to

Your Husky puppy will certainly be comfortable on your living room couch, but make sure he has plenty of opportunity to get out and about for socialization.

them gradually. For example, after your baby Siberian has had his vaccinations, take your puppy with you to the pet store when you go to buy some dog food. While there, introduce your puppy to the clerks, other customers, and even to the store parrot. Your trip there could also include walking up some stairs, walking on slippery floors, and going through an automatic door. All of these things, introduced gradually, with a lot of encouragement and repeated all over town, add up to a confident well-social-ized puppy.

During this time frame, pack instincts are developing and you can use this stage of growth to teach your puppy his position in the family. Each and every day, have each member of the family roll the puppy over and give him a tummy rub.

This exercise may seem very simple, but by baring his tummy, he is assuming a submissive position to family members. When his mom corrected him, he would roll over and bare his tummy to her; here, he's doing it for you.

When your baby Siberian is 11 and 12 weeks old, discipline becomes more important. Love, attention, and security are still vital, of course, but your puppy is now ready to learn some basic household rules. Don't allow him to do anything now, such as stealing food, jumping on people, or bouncing off the furniture, that you are not going to want him to do later, when he's full grown.

If your Siberian will not give up his toy after retrieving it, don't chase him or try to play tug-of-war. Establish yourself as pack leader so that he will play by your rules.

RETRIEVING

Begin retrieving games at 9 to 12 weeks of age. Throw a toy about six feet away and encourage him to chase it. When he grabs the toy, call him back. Praise him enthusiastically when he gives it to you. If he runs away and tries to turn it into a keep away game, stop playing. Don't chase him! Let him learn that he must play by your rules. Chasing a ball or Nylabone® Frisbee™ can be good exercise for your puppy and it sets the stage for a sound working relationship later.

THE THIRTEENTH THROUGH SIXTEENTH WEEK

From 13 through 16 weeks of age, your puppy will be trying to establish his position in your family pack. Consistency when enforcing the household rules is very important and everyone in the family should be doing things the same way. If he senses a soft heart or a weak link in the chain of command, he will take advantage of it.

Dominant personality puppies may start mounting behavior to small children or toys. This should be discouraged consistently—don't let it happen! Socialization with other people, dogs, and experiences should be continued.

Make sure the experiences are positive.

WEEKS SIXTEEN TO TWENTY SIX

Sometime between 16 and 20 weeks of age, many dogs go through another fear period, much like the one they had at eight weeks of age. Things the dog previously accepted as normal might become scary. A friend's Siberian Husky walked out into their backyard and started barking at a potted tree that had been there, in the same spot, since he was a baby. It was like he just suddenly noticed it and decided it was frightening!

During this fear stage, don't reinforce his fear. If you cuddle him and tell him, "It's okay, sweetie," he will assume that praise is for his reaction to the fear. In other words, you are praising the fear; the fear response was right! Instead, walk up to whatever is scaring him and touch it as you tell him, "Look at this." Walk him up to it if you can without frightening him too much. Help him overcome his fear instead of reinforcing it.

Many young Siberian Huskies discover their protective instincts at this time, too. If your puppy Siberian starts showing signs of protectiveness (growling, snarling, raised hackles) interrupt his behavior by distracting him or turning him away. If you encourage this behavior or correct it too harshly, you will put too much emphasis on it and your puppy may continue to do it. Too much emphasis may result in overprotectiveness or fearfulness in your dog as he grows up. Instead, react with calmness and just stop it from happening.

THE TEENAGE MONTHS

The teenage months in the life of dogs are very much like the teenage years in children. Kids in their teens are feeling strong, are striving to prove their ability to take care of themselves, and are trying to be independent. At the same time, they want the security of home. Those two conflicting needs seem to drive some teens (and their parents!) absolutely crazy! Dogs can be very much the same way—pushing the boundaries of their rules and testing you to see if you will enforce those rules. Many Siberian owners say that during this stage of growing up, their Siberians simply act "entirely too full of themselves!"

The teenage stage in Siberian Huskies hits at any time between 8 and 14 months of age and you will know when it

Your Siberian Husky puppy will soon grow into a large adult. You must teach and enforce household rules as soon as possible in order to avoid problems later.

Photo by Isabelle Francais.

Photo by Isabelle Francais.

During the teenage months, your Siberian will behave much like a child, challenging and defying your every command.

happens! One day you may ask your trained young dog to sit and he will act as if he has never heard the word before in his life! Your previously well-socialized dog may start barking or growling at other dogs or may start pushing your children around. You may have previously taught your Siberian to stay off the furniture, but during this stage, he may climb up there anyway and when you tell him to get off, he will either ignore you, or in extreme cases, may even growl at you!

You will need to consistently enforce your household rules during this stage. Hopefully you have already started obedience training and if you have, make sure you practice those skills regularly. If you have not yet started training, do so now. It's not too late.

Make sure your dog regards you as his leader. You can reinforce that idea by doing some things around the house. For example, you should always go through doors first. The dominant dog, alpha wolf, or leader of the pack always goes first. You should eat first, too. You should go up the stairs ahead of your dog; don't let him dash up the stairs and turn around and stare at you. If he does, he is assuming the dominant position!

Adolescent behavior is frustrating, but it is not directed at you personally. Your Siberian Husky is still a loyal and loving companion.

Siberian will grow up—some-day!

GROWING UP

Siberian Huskies are generally not considered fully mature—mentally and physically—until they are three years old. Sometimes the bitches (females) will mature a little earlier, at maybe two and a half years of age, but usually the dogs (males) take a little longer. After the teenage stage until they are grow up, your Siberian may go through some different behavioral stages. There may be another fear period—usually at about a year and a half of age.

Something else you can do is to give him permission to do things, even if he was going to do them anyway. For example, if he picks up his ball and is bringing it to you to throw, tell him, "Good boy to bring me your ball!" If he lies down at your feet, tell him, "Good boy to lie down!" By giving him permission and praising him, you are telling your dog that you have control.

It is very important you understand that your dog's adolescent behavior is natural—it is a part of growing up—and is not directed at you, personally. You must also remember that this, too, shall pass. Your

A puppy may be fearful or submissive in certain situations. Understand that this is just a phase that he will soon grow out of.

Handle this one just like you did the others; don't cater to your dog's fear, just work him through it.

There may be another period of challenging—seeing if you really are the boss—at about two years of age. Treat this as you did the teenage stage; enforce the rules and praise what he does right.

Sometimes there is a time when your Siberian may act somewhat territorial, protective, or even aggressive. Handle this just like you did when he was younger and do the same thing. Turn him away, distract him, or have him do something else, but don't overreact. If you do overreact and correct him too hard, he may get the wrong message— "Wow! Something is wrong!"— and that could cause his behavior to get worse.

When your Siberian Husky reaches the age of three years, he or she is generally considered to be grown up. However, grown up to a Siberian does not necessarily mean life is serious—no way! He may be serious when he needs to be or wants to be, but life to a Siberian is still great fun! So enjoy!

It's hard to imagine that this fun-loving youngster will ever grow up, but once your Siberian is three years old he is generally considered to be mature.

Photo by Isabelle Francais.

All About
FORMAL
Training

Many dog owners won't admit their dog needs training. "He does everything I ask," they say. Yet when asked specific questions about their dog's behavior, the answer changes. A trained dog is not going to jump on people, dash out the door each time it is opened, or raid the trash can.

Dog owners can benefit from training, too. Dog owners learn how to teach their dog, how to praise him, and how to motivate him to want to be good. They also learn how to prevent problem behavior from happening and how to correct the mistakes that do occur.

Dog training is much more than the traditional sit, down, stay, and come. Dog training means teaching your Siberian that he is living in *your* house, not his. It means that you can establish some household rules and that he is expected to follow those rules. It will not turn your Siberian into a little furry robot, but it will cause

Your Siberian needs the discipline and guidance that basic training can provide. This beauty takes a break from his lesson to pose for the camera.

Photo by Isabelle Francais.

Training makes everything you do with your pet more enjoyable, whether making a trip to the veterinarian or enjoying a quiet walk in the park.

your dog to look at you in a new light. Training will cause you to look at him a little differently, too. Dog training is not something you do to your Siberian; instead, it is something the two of you do together.

TRAINING METHODS

Talk to a dozen dog trainers (someone who trains dogs) or

Training classes not only teach your dog to act obediently, they give him a chance to socialize with other dogs. Apparently these adorable pups have yet to master the sit-stay command!

dog obedience instructors (someone who teaches the dog owner how to train his or her dog) and ask them how they train and you will get a dozen different methods. Any trainer

Photo by Isabelle Francais.

or instructor who has been in business for a period of time is going to work out a method that works for her. Each method will be based upon the trainer's personality, teaching techniques, experience, and philosophy regarding dogs and dog training. Any given method may work wonderfully for one trainer but should another trainer try the same things, it may fail terribly for her.

Because there are so many different techniques, styles, and methods, choosing a particular instructor can sometimes be difficult. It is important that you understand some of the different methods so that you can make a reasonable decision.

Compulsive Training

Compulsive training is regarded as a method of training that forces the dog to behave. This is usually a correction-based type of training, sometimes with forceful corrections. This training is often used for law enforcement and military dogs and can be quite effective for hard-driving, strong-willed dogs. In most cases, it is not the best training method for softer dogs. Many pet dog owners do

not like this style of training and often feel that it is too rough.

Inducive Training

This training is exactly the opposite of compulsive training. Instead of being forced to behave, the dog is induced or encouraged into the behavior. Depending upon the instructor, there are few or no corrections used. This training technique

Due to his industrious background and his eagerness to please his master, the Siberian Husky is very trainable. This Siberian gives his owner a high five for a job well done.

Photo by Isabelle Francais.

siberian husky

Photo by Isabelle Francais.

Inducive training employs few corrections and encourages your dog to behave correctly. This owner shapes his puppy into the down position.

THE MIDDLE ROAD

The majority of trainers and instructors use a training method that is somewhere in the middle between these two techniques. An inducive technique is used when possible, while corrections are used as needed. Obviously, the range can be vast, with some trainers leaning toward more corrections, while others use as few corrections as possible.

For most Siberians, this is the right training for them. A training method that is too rough or too compulsive will cause the dog to rebel. A training method without any compulsion will let the dog get away with too much. A training method that combines the better aspects of both methods will usually work very well for most Siberians.

works well for many puppies, for softer dogs, and sometimes for owners who dislike corrections of any kind. Unfortunately, this is not the technique for all dogs (especially all Siberian Huskies) because many Siberian Huskies are entirely too smart and will take advantage of the lack of corrections or discipline.

GROUP CLASSES OR PRIVATE LESSONS?

There are benefits and drawbacks to both group classes and private lessons. In group classes, the dog learns to behave around other distractions, specifically the other dogs and people in the class. Since the world is made up of lots of things capable of distracting your dog, this can work very well for most dogs and people. In addition, group classes work much like group therapy for the dog owners. The owners can share triumphs and mishaps and can encourage and support one another.

The drawback to group classes is that for some dogs

the distractions of the group class are too much. Some dogs simply cannot concentrate, especially in the beginning. For these dogs, a few private lessons may help enough so that the dog can join a group class later. Dogs with severe behavior problems—especially aggression towards other dogs or people—should also bypass group classes for obvious reasons.

Private lessons work well for dogs with specific problems, such as aggressive behavior. Private training is also good for dogs who are too distracted in a group setting or for dog

owners who are reluctant to speak up in a group class. The downfall of private training is the lack of distraction and for many instructors, the goal of private training is to get the dog and owner to the point that they can eventually join a group class.

WHAT ARE YOUR GOALS?

There are an unlimited number of things you can train your Siberian to do. It's up to you to decide what you would like to do and then find a training program to help you achieve those goals. Do you

Some dogs may need a few private lessons before they can deal with the distractions of a group class.

Photo by Alan Leschinski.

want to teach your dog to be a well-behaved house dog and companion? Do you want to compete in obedience trials? Would you like to do sledding or pulling competitions? Perhaps you would like to share your dog with others and participate in a therapy dog program. Think about your goals and then keep them in mind as you and your dog start training.

Puppy Class

Puppy or kindergarten classes are usually for puppies over 10 weeks of age and under 16 weeks of age. These classes are half training and half socialization. The puppy's owner learns how to housetrain his puppy, how to set up some household rules, and how to prevent problems from happening. The puppy learns some basic commands like sit and come. In addition, the puppy gets a chance to socialize and play with the people and puppies attending the class.

Basic Obedience Class

This class is usually for dogs over four months of age. In this class, the dogs and their owners work on the basic obedience commands, including sit, down, stay, heel, and come. Most

instructors also spend time discussing problem prevention and problem solving, especially the common problems like jumping on people, barking, digging, and chewing.

ADVANCED TRAINING

Advanced training classes vary in content depending upon the instructor. Some offer classes designed to teach your dog to work off leash, while others emphasize hand signals or other commands. Ask the instructor what she offers.

Dog Sports Training

Some instructors will offer classes preparing your dog to participate or compete in dog sports. These are the classes to take if you and your Siberian will be competing in obedience, agility, flyball, or other dog sports.

HOW TO FIND AN INSTRUCTOR OR TRAINER

When trying to find a trainer or instructor, word-of-mouth referrals are the best place to start. Although many instructors place an advertisement in the yellow pages or newspaper, anyone can place an ad and a fancy ad is no guarantee of expertise.

However, happy customers will demonstrate their experience with well-behaved dogs and will be glad to tell you where they received their instruction.

Have you admired a neighbor's well-behaved dog? Ask where they went for training. Call your veterinarian, local pet store, or groomer and ask who they recommend. Make notes about each referral. What did people like about this instructor and what did they dislike?

Once you have a list of referrals, start calling the instructors and ask a few questions. How long has she been teaching dog obedience classes? You will want someone with experience, of course, so that she is capable of handling different situations that may arise. However, experience alone is not the only qualification. Some people that have been teaching for years are still teaching exactly the same way and have never learned anything new.

Ask the instructor about Siberian Huskies—what does she think of the breed? Ideally, she should be knowledgeable about Siberian Huskies; what makes them tick and how to train them. If she doesn't like your breed, go elsewhere.

Photo by Alan Leschinski.

Choosing the right dog for your lifestyle was a big decision, and choosing the right trainer for your dog is just as important. Get referrals, observe classes and ask lots of questions!

Ask the instructor to describe her training methods. Does this sound like something you could be comfortable with? Ask if there are any alternative techniques used. Not every dog will respond to training the same way; every instructor should have alternative methods ready to use.

Does the instructor belong to any professional organizations? The National Association of Dog Obedience Instructors (NADOI) and the Association of Pet Dog Trainers (APDT) are two of the more prominent groups. Both of these publish regular newsletters to share information, techniques, new

Before committing to an obedience instructor, attend one of her classes to see if you would be comfortable with her teaching styles and methods.

developments, and more. Instructors that belong to professional organizations are more likely to be up-to-date on training techniques, styles, and so forth, as well as information about specific dog breeds.

Make sure that the instructor will be able to help you achieve your goals. If you want to compete in obedience, make sure she can either help you towards that end goal, or can refer you to someone else who can.

After talking to the instructors, ask if you can come watch one of their classes. If the instructor says no, then cross her off your list. There should be no reason why you cannot watch one class to see if you will be comfortable with this style of training. As you watch the class, watch how she handles the students' dogs. Would you let her handle your dog? How does she relate to the students? Are people relaxed? Are they paying attention to her? Do the students seem to be making progress?

After talking to the instructors and watching a class, you should be able to make a decision as to which class you wish to attend. If you are still undecided, call the instructors back and ask a few more questions. After all, you are hiring her to provide a service and you must be comfortable with your decision.

Early
PUPPY
Training

CRATE TRAINING

By about five weeks of age, most puppies are starting to toddle away from their mom and littermates to relieve themselves. You can use this instinct to keep their bed clean and with the help of a crate, housetrain your Siberian puppy.

A crate is a plastic or wire travel cage that you can use as your Siberian puppy's bed. Many new Siberian owners shudder at the thought of putting their puppy in a cage. "I could never do that!" they say, "It would be like putting my children in jail!" A puppy is not a child, however, and has different needs and instincts. Puppies like to curl up in small close places. That's why they like to sleep under the coffee table or under a chair.

Because your Siberian puppy does have an instinct to keep his bed clean, being confined in the crate will help him develop

Crate training is the fastest and easiest way to housebreak your Siberian Husky.

Photo by Isabelle Francais.

more bowel and bladder control. When he is confined for gradually extended periods of time, he will hold his wastes to avoid soiling his bed. It is your responsibility to make sure he is never left for too long.

The crate will also be your Siberian puppy's place of refuge. If he's tired, hurt, or sick, allow him to go back to his crate to sleep or hide. If he's overstimulated or excited, put him back in his crate to calm down. Because the crate physically confines the puppy, it can prevent some unwanted behaviors, such as chewing on electrical cords or slippers.

Introducing the Crate

Introduce your puppy to the crate by propping open the door and tossing a treat inside. As you do this, tell your puppy, "Go to bed!" and let him go in to get the treat. Let him investigate the crate and go in and out freely. When your puppy will go in after the treat and has sniffed the crate thoroughly, offer a meal in the crate with the door propped open. The next meal can be offered in the crate and this time, close the door behind him, but let him out as soon as he has finished eating. Offer several meals in the same fashion in order to show your puppy that the crate is a pretty neat place.

BLANK SLATE

A puppy is like a blank slate or in modern terms, a blank, newly formatted computer disk, ready for you to write on. What you teach the puppy in his early months will have bearing on the rest of the puppy's life. Therefore, it's important to keep in your mind a vision of what your dog will grow up to be. Although Siberian Huskies are medium-sized dogs, they are still very strong for their size, and you need to keep this in mind as you train your puppy. At ten weeks of age, your Siberian puppy would love to cuddle on your lap, but will you really want him to do that when he's 55 pounds of muscle, hard elbows, and tough feet? Some people may enjoy this, but others may prefer having the dog cuddle at their feet instead. By establishing some basic rules early, your puppy grows up understanding these rules. You can prevent potential problems from developing later.

After your puppy is calm eating in the crate, start feeding his meals back in the normal location and go back to offering him a treat or toy for going into the crate. Continue teaching him the phrase, "Go to bed."

Don't let your puppy out of the crate after having a temper tantrum. If he starts crying, screaming, throwing himself or scratching at the door, correct him verbally, "No! Quiet!" or simply close the bedroom door and walk away. If you let him out after a temper tantrum, you will just teach him that temper tantrums work! Instead, let him out when you are ready and when he is quiet.

Crate Location

The ideal place for the crate is in your bedroom within arm's reach of the bed. This will give him eight uninterrupted hours with you while you do nothing but sleep. In these busy times, that is quality time! Having you nearby will also give your puppy a feeling of security. If you exile him to the backyard or garage, he will be more apt to cry, whine, howl, pace, or get into trouble because of loneliness and fear. Instead, keep him close.

Having your puppy close at night will also save you some wear and tear. If he needs to go outside, you will hear him and can let him out before he has an accident. If he's restless or bored, you can rap the top of his crate and tell him to be quiet.

HOUSETRAINING

One of the most common methods of training a puppy is paper training. The puppy is taught to relieve himself on newspaper and then, at some point, is retrained to go outside. Paper training teaches the puppy to relieve himself in the house. Is that really what you want your Siberian to know?

Teach your puppy what you want him to know. Take him outside to the area where you want him to relieve himself and tell him, "Go potty!" (Use any command comfortable for you.)

Despite the fact that paper training is one of the most common methods of housebreaking, it can actually confuse your puppy by teaching him that it is acceptable to relieve himself in the house.

Photo by Isabelle Francais.

Photo by Isabelle Francais.

When introducing your Siberian puppy to his crate, leave the door open so that he may go in and out freely to investigate this new area.

siberian husky

When he has done what he needed to do, praise him, "Good boy to go potty!" Don't just send your Siberian puppy out into the backyard and hope that he does what he needs to do; you may let him back into the house just to see him squat on the rug! You need to go with him to see that he has relieved himself in the correct area so that you can praise him for doing so!

Successful housetraining is based upon setting your puppy up for success rather than failure. Keep accidents to a minimum and praise him when he does relieve himself where he should go.

Establish a Routine

Your Siberian puppy is a creature of habit; routines are very important. Housetraining is much easier if there is a set routine for eating, eliminating, playing, walking, and sleeping. A workable schedule might look like this:

• **6:00 am**—Dad wakes up and takes the puppy outside. After the puppy relieves himself and dad praises him, dad fixes the puppy's breakfast, offers him water and then takes him back outside.

• **7:00 am**—Mom goes outside to play with the puppy before getting ready for work. Just before she leaves, she

Like most puppies, this adorable Siberian Husky enjoys eating and resting in a small enclosed space.

Photo by Isabelle Francais.

Crating should be an enjoyable experience for your pup. These two take the opportunity to compete for top dog!

brings the puppy inside and puts him in his crate and gives him a treat.

• **11:00 am**—A dog-loving neighbor who is retired comes over, lets the puppy out of his crate and takes him outside. The neighbor knows the puppy's training, so he praises him when he relieves himself. He throws the ball for the puppy, pets and cuddles him, and then gives him a treat when he puts him back in his crate.

• **3:00 pm**—Daughter comes home from school and lets the puppy out into the backyard

while she changes clothes. After calling her friends on the phone, she goes out back with the puppy, throws the ball, cleans up the yard a little, and then takes the puppy for a walk. When they get back, she brings the puppy to her bedroom while she works on her homework.

• **6:00 pm**—Mom takes the puppy outside to go potty, praises him, and then feeds him dinner.

• **8:00 pm**—After daughter plays with the puppy, she takes him back outside.

PUNISHMENT

If you try to housetrain your puppy by punishing him for accidents that happen in the house, either by rubbing his nose in his mess (a commonly used correction) or by sharply scolding him, you run the risk of confusing him more than teaching him. If you correct your puppy for housetraining accidents, he may feel that going potty is what is wrong and he may start being sneaky about where he goes so that you can't catch him. You may start finding "surprises" in strange locations around the house or yard. Keep in mind that the act of relieving himself is not what is wrong—he has to do that—instead, it is relieving himself in the house that is the problem.

• **11:00 pm**—Dad takes the puppy out for one more chance to go potty before going to bed.

The schedule you establish will have to work with your normal routine and lifestyle. Just keep in mind that the puppy should not remain in his crate for longer than three to four hours, except at night. The puppy will need to relieve himself after eating and drinking, after exercise and playtime, and when waking up from a nap.

If you allow your Siberian Husky to develop bad habits like sitting on furniture as a youngster, it will be hard to break him of these habits as he matures.

Photo by Isabelle Francais.

Limit the Puppy's Freedom

Many puppies do not want to take the time to go outside to go potty, especially if there are interesting things happening in the house. Those puppies will then sneak off somewhere—a back bedroom or behind the sofa—to relieve themselves. By limiting the puppy's freedom you can prevent these "accidents" from happening. Close bedroom doors and use baby gates across hallways to keep your puppy close. If you can't keep an eye on him, put him outside or in his crate.

Household Rules

It's important to start establishing some household rules as soon as your new puppy joins your household. Your puppy, at eight to ten weeks of age, is not too young to learn and by starting early you can prevent problems from getting started. When deciding what rules you want to establish, look at your puppy, not as the baby he is now but rather the adult he will grow up to be. You may not mind if your Siberian puppy is on the couch now, but are you going to want him up there when he's fully grown? Do you want him jumping on people? A full-grown Siberian is strong enough to knock over toddlers, scratch legs, rip panty hose, and ruin clothes.

Some common household rules might include teaching your puppy not to jump on people, to behave when guests come over, to stay out of the kitchen, and not to chew on inappropriate things. In addition, you might want to teach the puppy to leave the kids' toys alone, to ignore dirty clothes, and to stay off the furniture.

To teach your puppy what is and is not allowed, you must be very clear with your commands and corrections. Either something is right or it is wrong. When the puppy picks up his toy instead of your slippers, praise him, "Good boy to play with your toy!" When he picks up your slipper, correct him, "No! That's not yours!" Take the slipper away and then give him one of his toys, "Here this is your toy!" Let him know what is wrong, then follow it by showing him what he can do instead and praise him when he does it.

ACCEPTING THE LEASH

All dogs need to accept the restraints of a leash, although this can be hard for some puppies. If your Siberian puppy is frightened by the leash as a baby, he may resent the leash

Keeping your Siberian on a consistent feeding schedule will aid in successful housetraining.

Photo by Isabelle Francais.

for the rest of his life. Therefore you want to introduce the leash calmly and positively.

Photo by Isabelle Francais.

When you and your Siberian Husky are outdoors, keep him on leash for his safety, as well as the safety of others.

PRACTICE PATIENCE

New puppy owners seem to invite advice. Everyone has a method of housetraining that works better or faster and is more reliable than anyone else's method. Ignore your well-meaning friends. Siberian puppies need time to grow up and develop bowel and bladder control. Establish a routine that works well for you and stick with it. If you stick with the schedule, your puppy will progress. However, don't let apparent success go to your head; don't *assume* he is housetrained. Too much freedom too soon will result in problems.

Soon after you bring your puppy home, put a soft nylon or cotton buckle collar on him. Make sure it's loose enough to slip over his head should he get tangled up with something (as Siberian puppies are known to do!). After a day or two, when he is no longer scratching at the collar, attach a leash to the collar and let him drag it around the house for 10 or 15 minutes while you watch him to make sure it doesn't tangle on something. While the puppy is dragging the leash, he will step on the leash, feel the tug on his neck, and just generally get used to the feel of it.

After two or three sessions of dragging the leash, you can teach your puppy to follow you when you have the leash in hand. Have a few pieces of a soft treat you know he likes, such as a hot dog or cheese. Let him sniff the treat and then back away while you verbally encourage him, "Let's go! Good boy!" When he follows you for a few feet, stop, praise him, and let him have a bite of the treat. Siberian Huskies are the original proverbial food hounds and training with treats for these dogs makes training much easier!

Repeat the exercise two or three times and quit for this session. Reward your puppy by throwing the tennis ball a few times. After two or three training sessions like this, start making it more challenging by backing away from your puppy faster or by adding turns or zigzags. If he balks or acts confused, stop and go back to the simple back away again until he understands.

PRAISE

Never stop the training session when your Siberian puppy is confused. Instead, always end the training session on a high note. Do something you know he can do well then stop, praise him enthusiastically and play ball with him for a few minutes.

INTRODUCING THE CAR

Many puppies are frightened by car rides because the car took them away from mom and their littermates and the car takes them to the veterinarian's office where scary things happen. You don't want this idea to blossom, though—you want your puppy to understand that riding in the car can be a good thing.

Start by lifting your puppy into the car and handing him a good treat. As soon as he has eaten the treat, lift him down and walk away. Repeat that sporadically over several days. Then lift him into the car, give him a treat, let him eat it and explore the car a little. After he has sniffed a little, give him another treat, let him eat it, and lift him out of the car. Continue this type of training for a week or more, depending upon how nervous your puppy is about the car.

Treats are a great tool for training; use them to praise your pup, as well as to entice him into performing his tricks.

When your puppy is expecting a treat in the car, then take his crate, put it in the car, and strap it down so that it

Photo by Isabelle Francais.

If your Siberian is to compete in dog shows, he must become accustomed to extensive traveling.

won't bounce around or go flying in an emergency situation. Put your puppy in his crate, give him a treat and close the crate door and the car door. Start the engine, back the car out of the driveway and then drive back up to the house. Give your puppy a treat and let him out of the crate. The next time, drive down the street and back, then around the block. Increase the time and distance of the drives very gradually.

Keep in mind that you want your puppy to anticipate good things in the car. Your dog will have a lifetime of car rides ahead of him and life will be much nicer if he can enjoy the rides.

SOCIAL HANDLING

Your puppy cannot care for himself; you must be able to brush him, pull burrs and foxtails out of his coat, clean his ears, and trim his nails. Unfortunately, your Siberian puppy doesn't understand that cleaning his ears is necessary and he may struggle and fight when you try to do these things. The social handling exercise will help teach your puppy to accept your care.

Sit on the floor and have your puppy lie down between

Aaaah! Tummy rubs are good for pet and owner alike, as they relax an excited dog, familiarize him with your touch, and serve as bonding time.

massage. Start at his neck and ears and gently massage the muscles. Work down his neck to his shoulders, down each front leg to the paw. Touch the paw gently but firmly (some dogs are ticklish) and touch each toenail. Go back to his body and massage the back, the ribcage, and the hips. Work down the back legs just like you did his front legs. And then give his tail a little massage as well.

Once your puppy has learned to enjoy this handling, you can—during the massage— check his ears and clean them when needed, brush him, check for fleas or ticks, trim his toenails, comb out burrs, or even medicate him when necessary.

your legs. He can lie on his back or his side and he can get comfortable. Start by giving him a slow, easy tummy rub; the idea here is to relax him. If he starts to wiggle or struggle, gently restrain him with one hand as you massage him with the other.

When the puppy is no longer struggling, start giving him a

CALMING DOWN
This social handling can even be used to calm an excited or overstimulated puppy. If you let your puppy in from the backyard and he is bouncing off the walls with excitement and energy, you have a couple of choices. If you try to correct the puppy, he will probably just get more excited. However, if you grab him, lay him down, and start massaging him, he will relax. In addition, you are giving him the attention he wants and needs from you.

The Basic
OBEDIENCE
Commands

TEACHING YOUR SIBERIAN HUSKY

Teaching your Siberian is a process. Unfortunately you cannot simply tell your dog to sit and expect him to do it. First of all, until he has been taught what the word "sit" means, it is simply an unknown sound. To confuse training even more, he has no idea why you want him to sit or does he know why it is so important to you. Therefore, teaching becomes a process.

You want to show your dog what it is you want him to do. Help shape him into the sit if that is what you are teaching, or move him off the furniture if that is your focus. Then, as you are helping him, teach him the word, "Sit" or "Off the furniture." Praise him when he does it right, even if you have helped him. "Good boy to sit!" or "Good boy to get off the furniture!"

Praise him every time he does something right. Your dog will work harder and do more for you when you use a lot of praise. That doesn't mean that you should give undeserved praise; even your dog can figure

that out. Instead, give enthusiastic praise when he makes an effort and does something right for you.

Interrupt incorrect behavior or actions as your dog is thinking about it or starts to move. If you have asked him to sit and he does, but then starts to sniff and lean as if he is going to get up, interrupt him, "Don't do it!" When he looks at you, tell him, "That's good to sit!"

BE FAIR

Make sure you are very clear as to what you want from your dog. Remember, to your dog something is either right or wrong; it's not partially right or partially wrong. Be fair with your demands, your praise, and your corrections.

Interruptions and corrections will not teach your dog; they are used only to stop—at that moment—undesirable behavior or actions. Your dog learns much more when you reward his good behavior. So stop what you don't want, but lavishly praise what you do want!

Timing is vitally important as you teach your dog. Make sure

The sit is a very basic command, but it serves as the foundation for many future exercises. This trainer places her right hand on her dog's chest as she slides her left hand down his back to his rump, gently shaping him into the sit.

you praise him as he is doing something right and interrupt or correct him as he is making a mistake.

> ### DON'T PRACTICE INCORRECT BEHAVIOR
> Do not correct your dog for not cooperating until you are sure he understands what it is you are asking him to do. Once he understands and is willing do it, then when he chooses not to, you can correct him with a verbal correction or a quick snap and release of the leash. Use *only* as much correction as needed to get his attention and *no more*. With corrections, less is better!

SIT AND RELEASE

The sit is the foundation command for everything else you will teach your Siberian. When your Siberian learns to sit and sit still, he is also learning to control himself. Learning self-control is a very hard lesson for many young Siberian Huskies—being still is simply not in their genetic code! However, your Siberian can learn to control himself and the sit is the place to start.

The sit is also the foundation command for many other exercises, including the lie down and wait, as well as many advanced obedience commands. The sit is also great around the house. Your Siberian cannot jump up on people for petting if he is sitting. He cannot knock his food bowl out of your hand at dinner time if he's sitting. You can fasten his leash to his collar more easily if he is sitting still. It's a useful command!

There are two methods used to teach your Siberian to sit. Some methods work better for some dogs than they do for others, so try both and see which will be better. Hold your Siberian's leash in your left hand and have some treats in your right hand. Tell your Siberian to sit as you move your right hand (and the treats) from his nose over his head towards his tail. He will lift his head to follow your hand and will sit in response to that movement. As he sits, praise him, "Good boy to sit!" Pet him while he's in the sitting position, give him a treat, and have him hold the sit until you pat him on the shoulder to

Have your Husky develop a good habit; make him sit before receiving any treats or petting.

release him, "Release!" We want this release command to tell your dog that he is finished with that particular exercise and can move. You will be using the release with several different exercises.

If your dog is too excited by treats to concentrate on sitting, or if he spins around in place to get the treat instead of sitting, then try the second technique. Tell your Siberian to sit as you put your right hand on the front of his chest and your left hand slides down his back to his rump as you gently shape him into a sit. Praise him for sitting, pet him quietly, and do not allow him to pop back up. If he does, shape him back into position. If he is very wiggly, keep your hands on him as you praise him for sitting, then, with your hands on him, you can gently restrain him so that he cannot pop back up. When you are ready for him to move from the sit, pat him on the shoulder, and tell him, "Release!"

Don't get into the habit of repeating your commands. If you tell your dog to sit three or four times, which one should he listen to? You are not teaching him sit by repeating it, but you are teaching him that he doesn't have to listen to you. Is that really what you want him

One way to teach the down command is to hold a treat in front of your Husky's paws and take it down to the ground. As he follows the treat, he will inevitably end up in the down position.

to learn? Instead, give each command only once and then help your dog to succeed. Tell him to sit, wait a heartbeat to allow him to do it, and if he doesn't, help him do it.

DOWN

The down exercise continues one of the lessons the sit exercise started—self-control. It is hard for many young bouncy Siberian Huskies to control their own actions, but it's a lesson that all must learn. Teaching and practicing the down exercise teaches your Siberian to lie down and be still.

Start with your Siberian in a sit. Rest one hand gently on his shoulders and have a treat in

An alternative method for teaching the down is to simply scoop your Husky's front legs up and down, and shape him into position. Once down, have him hold the position for a few seconds, then release and give praise generously.

the other hand. Let him smell the treat and then tell him, "Dog, lie down" as you take the treat straight down to the ground in front of his front paws. As he follows the treat to the ground, use your hand on his shoulders to encourage him to lie down. Praise him, give him the treat, have him hold the position for a few moments, and then release in the same manner that you did from the sit. Pat him on the shoulder and tell him, "Release!"

If your Siberian looks at the treat as you make the signal but doesn't follow the treat to the ground, simply scoop his front legs up and forward and lay him down. The rest of the exercise is the same.

As your Siberian learns what down means, you can have him hold it for a few seconds longer before you release him, but do not step away from him. Stay next to him and if you need to, keep a hand on his shoulder to encourage him to remain down.

STAY

When you taught your Siberian to sit and to lie down, you taught him to move into those positions and to hold still until you released him. The stay command continues those exercises by teaching your dog to continue to hold still for gradually increasing times as you move away from him. Eventually your Siberian will be able to hold the sit or down stay for several minutes (longer in the down) and when you are a distance away, maybe even in another room.

Start by having your Siberian sit. With the leash in your left hand, use the leash to put a slight bit of pressure backwards (towards his tail) as you tell him, "Dog, stay." At the same time, use your right hand to give your dog a signal that will mean stay—an open hand gesture with the palm towards your dog's face. Take one step away and at the same time, release the pressure on the

If your Siberian breaks his stay, simply correct him verbally and place him back into position.

The stay exercise can be a continuation of the down; your dog remains in his down for increasing amounts of time.

leash. If your Siberian moves towards you, gets up or lies down, tell him "No" (so that he understands he has made a mistake) and put him back into position. Repeat the exercise. After a few seconds—and a few seconds only—step back to your dog and praise him. Don't let him move from position until you give him the release command.

You can use the same process to teach your dog to stay in the down position. Have him sit, then lie down. Give him the verbal command to stay and the hand signal while putting slight pressure

Photo by Alan Leschinski.

backward on the leash. Step one step away as you release pressure on the leash. If he moves, tell him "No" and put him back into position. After a few seconds, go back to him, praise him, and then release him.

With the stay command, you always want to go back to your dog to release him. Don't release him from a distance or call him to come from the stay. If you do either of these, your dog will be much less reliable on the stay; he will continue to get up from the stay or will start to anticipate the release from a distance. When teaching the stay, you want your dog to understand that stay means "Hold this position until I go back to you and release you." No confusion and no questions asked.

As your dog learns the stay command, you can increase the time he holds the stay. However, make sure you increase the time very gradually. If your dog is making a lot of mistakes, such as moving often, you are either asking your dog to hold the stay too long or your dog doesn't understand the command yet. In either case, go back and teach the command from the beginning, very gradually

increasing the time you ask him to hold the stay.

Increase the distance you move away from your dog just as gradually. Again, if your dog is making a lot of mistakes, make sure he understands what you are asking him to do. Then, increase the distance one step away at a time.

SOCIAL GRACES OF THE STAY COMMAND

When your Siberian has learned the basics on the stay, start using the down stay around the house. Have your dog down stay while you are eating so that he isn't begging under the table or stealing food from the kids. Have him do a down stay when people come over so he isn't jumping all over your guests. There are a lot of practical uses for this command; just look at your normal routine and see where they can work for you and then use them.

Once your Siberian understands the stay command and you know that he understands it, you can start correcting mistakes. As has been mentioned before (and will be mentioned again!) young Siberian Huskies are wiggly bouncy creatures that have a hard time holding still. Self-control is a skill that must be learned. If your Siberian is having a hard time holding still, keep the stay short in time and distance. Correct excess movement with a sharp verbal correction and a snap and release of the leash. When your dog does hold the stay, especially when he has been having a hard time, praise him enthusiastically!

WATCH ME

The watch me exercise is a very useful command that teaches your Siberian to ignore distractions and focus on you. This will be particularly useful when you and your dog are out in public and he gets excited by children playing, dogs barking, or birds flying overhead.

The watch me exercise teaches your Siberian Husky to ignore distractions and focus solely on you.

Photo by Alan Leschinski.

Start by having your dog sit in front of you. With the leash in your left hand, have a treat in your right hand. Let your dog smell the treat and then take it up to your chin as you tell him, "Dog, watch me!" When his eyes follow your hand to your face and he looks at you, praise him, "Good boy to watch me!" Give him the treat and release him from the sit. This is a particularly hard exercise for many young Siberian Huskies, so teach it first in the house with few distractions. Make sure your dog can do it and understands it well before moving on to the next step.

When he will watch you while you practice in the house, then move outside where there are more distractions. If he knows the command and ignores you, take his chin in your left hand as you give the signal with your right. Help him to look at you. If he still struggles against you, use a verbal correction. When he looks back at you, praise him.

When your dog will watch you outside with a few distractions, you can move on to the next training step. Start with your dog sitting in front of you, give him the command "Watch me," and then start walking backwards. Encourage him to follow you and watch you at the same time. After six steps (or so) stop and have him sit, then praise him enthusiastically! After a few tries, back up a little farther, then add turns and zigzags. Make it challenging and when he can watch you, make the praise worthwhile—tell him what a wonderful dog he is!

HEEL

When your Siberian can watch you while you walk backwards, then you are ready to teach the heel. Heel will mean, "Walk with me, by my left side, with your neck and shoulders by my left leg. You will pay attention to me and walk as I do; slow, fast, normal, left turns, right turns, and anything else." Obviously, this is a complicated exercise. However, if your Siberian is watching well, it won't be too hard.

To first start it, practice a watch me exercise as you have been doing it by backing away from your dog. When he is following you well and paying attention, simply turn your body—as you are walking—so that you and your dog end up walking forward together with him on your left side. Picture this in your mind—you are backing away from your dog, your dog is facing you, following you. Go back to your dog's right as you continue walking. You and your dog should be facing the same direction with your dog on your left. This is the heel. When you stop, have your dog sit.

If, while you are walking, your dog starts to pull forward, simply back away from him and encourage him to follow you

Guaranteed by the manufacturer to stop any dog, any size, any weight from ever pulling again. It's like having power steering for your dog. Photo courtesy of Four Paws.

again. If you need to, use the leash to make sure he follows you quickly. Praise him when he does. When his attention is back on you, turn into the heel position again. Don't be upset if you have to back away a few times. In fact, the more you do it, the better. Your dog will pay more attention to you if he's not quite sure where you will be going.

When your dog is walking with you nicely, then you can start eliminating the backing away. Start the heel with your dog sitting on your left side and tell him, "Watch me! Dog, heel!" and start walking. Praise him when he's walking nicely with you. If he starts to pull, you can correct him, "Dog, no pull!" However, if he is intent upon pulling or is distracted, simply back away from him and turn him away from whatever is distracting him.

COME

With a Treat

The come command is one of the most important commands your Siberian Husky will learn. Not only is the come command important around the house and yard, but if he should be out in front of your house, the come could save him

Your Siberian will be a tractable companion on your daily walks when he learns to heel.

from dashing into the street and getting hit by a car. If you take him out to run or decide to do skijoring or sled dog work with him, he must have a good, reliable come.

Because the come command is so important, you will use two different techniques for teaching it. The first method will use food treats to teach your Siberian that the come is fun and will result in a treat—something near and dear to all Siberian Huskies! Take a small plastic container, like a small margarine container, and put some dog food kibble in it so that it makes a nice plastic rattling sound. Then, have some treats in hand that you know your dog really likes—something special. Shake the container and ask your dog if he wants a treat, using the word he already knows for treat, such as cookie, biscuit, or bone. "Dog, do you want a cookie?" Then pop a treat in his mouth. This, combined with shaking the container, teaches your dog that the sound of the container equals a treat. Do this for several days until your dog comes running whenever he hears the container rattling.

At that point, you can shake the container and say, "Dog, Cookie! Come!" This builds a relationship between the words cookie and come. After a few days, drop the word cookie altogether and simply shake the container, saying, "Dog, come!" and pop a treat in his mouth.

Practice this command two or three times per training session, several times a day. Don't do it too many times in a session or it will lose its appeal. However, you do need to practice it a lot so that the dog reacts to it automatically, without even thinking about what he's doing.

After making eye contact, call your dog by name and give the command to come. Remember to praise him when he comes to you.

siberian husky

Training sessions can sometimes become long and frustrating, so be sure to take frequent breaks and give praise and affection for a job well done.

USE IT OR LOSE IT!

The best way to make this obedience training work for you and your Siberian is to use it. Training is not just for those training sessions; instead, training is for daily life. Incorporate the training into your daily routine. Have your Siberian sit for dinner and for treats. Have him lay down and stay during meals or when company comes over. Have him sit and stay at doorways so that he isn't dashing out open doors. Use these commands and make them a part of your life. They will work better that way.

Eyes on the prize!—Training with a treat will make any Husky attentive.

Some people that have reservations about this technique are worried that their dog will not come to them when they don't have a treat. First of all, you will be using two different techniques to teach your Siberian to come for that express reason. Later, when your dog is coming reliably every time you call him, you will be able to get rid of the treats, although it is important to use them as long as you need them. In addition, this technique—when taught properly—can produce such a wonderful, strong reliable come that it is worth all your efforts.

With the Long Line

The second method will teach your dog to come when he's a little farther away from you. It will also help teach your Siberian to come to you on those instances when you don't have the treat container.

With this technique, you will need a 20- to 30-foot length of cotton clothesline rope. Don't use nylon—it is too rough on your hands. Fasten the rope to your dog's collar and let him go play. When he is distracted by a bird or his toys, call him, "Dog (his name), come!" If he comes to you right away, praise him enthusiastically. If he does not come directly to you, do *not* call him again. Simply pick up the rope, back away from him, and using the rope, make him come to you. Now the key to this is to verbally praise him, even if you have to drag him in to you. The come has got to be positive; if he thinks he's going to get into trouble by coming to you, he won't come at all. So you have to praise him. Let the long line be the bad guy.

After you have praised him, release him and let him go play again. In a few minutes, repeat the exercise all over again. Practice this in the back and front yard, even in the house if he plays keep away in the house. Teach your dog that he must come to you the first time you call him, every time you call him.

Don't allow your Siberian freedom off leash in an unfenced area until he is well trained, grown up, and mentally mature enough to handle that responsibility. Many dog owners let their dogs off leash much too soon and the dog learns that he can run away from them or play keep away, staying just out of reach. And Siberians so love to run! Each time he does this, he learns that he can and there is nothing you can do to change his mind. Therefore, leave him on leash or on a long line until he is properly trained and grown up. For some Siberian Huskies, that might be two and a half or three years old.

When teaching the come command, keep your Husky on his leash. You may have to pull him toward you if he doesn't obey.

Photo by Alan Leschinski.

This happy Husky gives his owner an enthusiastic thank you for all of her consistent and patient training.

Advanced
TRAINING
and Dog Sports

One of the great things about dog training is that you are never finished; there is always more you can teach your dog. Would you like your Siberian to behave himself off leash? You can teach him that. Wouldn't teaching him to recognize and respond to some hand signals be fun? It is. Your dog can learn hand signals for down, sit, stand, stay, and more, including directions left and right. How about pulling a sled, a skier, or a wagon?

Before you start teaching your Husky any of these commands, make sure he is proficient at his basic commands. He should be able to respond to the sit, down, stay, and heel (on leash) with one command and very few corrections. Ideally, he should also come to you when you call (off leash in the house or fenced yard) using the shaker and a verbal command. If your dog is still having some trouble with the basics, work on those some

Obedience training takes a lot of work, but it tremendously enhances the relationship between a dog and his owner.

more before going on to these commands.

HAND SIGNALS

When you start teaching your Siberian hand signals, use a treat in your hand to get his attention and use the verbal command he already knows to help him understand what you want. As he responds better and starts to show some understanding of the command, you can then make the verbal command softer and eventually stop saying it.

The difficult part of teaching your dog hand signals is that in the beginning, he may not understand that there is some significance in your motions. After all, people move their hands constantly, especially when they are talking, and your dog may not realize that those motions could mean something. Also, for hand signals to work, your dog must be watching you!

Down

When you taught your Siberian to lie down by taking a treat to the ground in front of his feet, you were starting to teach him a hand signal. Granted, he was watching the treat in your hand, but he was also getting used to seeing your hand take the treat there. That

motion of your hand is a signal; a command that can mean the same thing as your verbal command, "Down." Continue using the treat in the beginning; don't get rid of the treat until you are sure that he knows the signal and is following the hand signal reliably.

DAILY USES

Some people teach advanced obedience commands for competition or other dog sports, which we'll talk more about later in this chapter. But some of these commands are great for your daily life with your dog. For example, if your dog responds to hand signals, you can give him the signal to go lie down and stay while you are talking on the telephone. That way you won't interrupt your conversation.

Start teaching him by practicing the down with the signal as you taught him earlier. Have him sit, tell him, "Down" and take the treat to the ground in front of him. When he's down, praise him and release him. If he's doing this well, with no hesitation, give him the signal and delay your whispered verbal command by a couple seconds. If he lies down for your signal, praise him enthusiastically! If he waits for your verbal command, try it again with more emphasis on the signal.

When he can follow the signal with no verbal command, start making it more challenging. Continue to have him sit, but stand in front of him and then signal him to lie down. Walk a leash length away and try it. Try it from across the room. Remember to praise him enthusiastically when he follows your signal and lies down.

Do not allow your Siberian Husky off-leash freedom until you are positive he will consistently and dependably obey you.

Sit

If you were able to teach your Siberian to sit using the treat above his nose, you were starting to teach him a signal that means sit. If you weren't able to use that technique, don't worry—he can still learn a sit signal.

With your Siberian on the leash held in your left hand, have a treat in your right hand and standing in front of him, take the treat from his nose up to your left shoulder so that your forearm is up and across your chest. At the same time, tell him, "Dog, sit" in a soft voice. If he hesitates, give him a jiggle of the leash and collar. If he refuses, tell him to sit again and snap and release the leash. When he sits, praise him, give

him the treat, release him, and try it again.

Stay

As you taught your Siberian the stay command earlier, you were again introducing him to a hand signal. When you said, "Dog, stay" and put your open palm in front of his nose, that was a hand signal. In fact, this signal is so obvious your dog will probably obey it right away with little extra training. Try it by having your dog sit, then give him the stay signal without a verbal command and see what happens. Did he hold it? If he did, go back to him and praise him. If he didn't, put him back where he started, give him the signal again, and quietly tell him to stay.

Come

The come signal will start with your right hand and arm straight out to your side at shoulder height. Bring it around to your chest as if you were reaching out to get your dog and bringing him to you. Finish it by making the sit signal; up and across your chest, so that when your Siberian comes dashing to you, he will see the sit signal and sit in front of you.

Start teaching it by having the come shaker in your right hand and shake it slightly as you make the arm signal and quietly tell your dog to come. You may also need to quietly tell your dog to sit as you finish with the sit command. He isn't used to watching more than one command at a time. When he comes and sits, praise him enthusiastically and give him a treat.

Watch your dog and when he seems to understand the signal, take away the shaker and practice the signal with a quiet verbal command. Continue to pop a treat in his mouth when he does come. Gradually eliminate the verbal command but continue to praise and reward him for coming to you.

Hand signals in conjunction with verbal commands can be very useful when training your Husky.

Photo by Alan Leschinski.

OFF-LEASH CONTROL

One of the biggest mistakes people make with their dogs is to take them off the leash too soon. When your dog is off leash, you have very little (or no) control and your dog will learn very quickly that he can get away from you and there's nothing you can do about it. Siberian Huskies are very inquisitive dogs and love to explore. More than one Siberian has gotten so involved in his exploring that he has forgotten he should have been paying attention to his owner. Worse yet, these dogs love to run and will run too far, too fast.

Before he is allowed total off-leash freedom (outside of your house or fenced-in yard) you need to make sure that his training is sound. That means he understands the basic commands and responds to them reliably.

Your Siberian Husky must also be mentally mature enough to handle the responsibility of off-leash freedom. Mentally mature means that he is through the adolescent challenging stage of growing up. Most Siberian Huskies are not mentally adult until they are two and a half or three years old, some even older. Until then they are still very puppy-like

and don't take anything seriously. There's nothing wrong with this—many people love puppies, even big puppies! However, puppies do not have the concentration, responsibility, and seriousness to be allowed off-leash freedom.

USING THE HAND SIGNALS

When your dog has a good understanding of the hand signals, you can start putting them together and using them in groups as part of your training sessions. Have your Siberian come, sit, lie down, and then come again. Praise him enthusiastically and reward him with a treat. Or rearrange the order: have him lie down, then come back up to a sit, then come and lie down again. Challenge your training skills and his learning and attention skills.

The Long Leash and the Come Command

The long leash that was introduced earlier in the section on teaching the come command is a good training tool for teaching off-leash control. Before, you used the long leash to teach your dog to come to you when he was at a distance (but within reach of the long leash) from you. Review that training session by

Photo by Alan Leschinski.

You should be able to trust your dog to remain where he is commanded to stay while you are out of sight. Reinforce the stay at every opportunity.

putting your Siberian on the long leash and while holding one end of it, let him go play. When he is distracted and not paying attention to you, call him to come and back away from him so that he gets a chance to chase you. (The chase is exciting to most dogs and this will make the come more exciting.) If he doesn't immediately start to come to you, use the long leash to give him a snap and release. If he is still ignoring you, reel him in like a fish on a fishing pole. When he gets to you, either under his own power or yours, you must praise him. The come must be rewarded; however, if

he comes to you voluntarily, the praise should be much more enthusiastic!

Heel

In most public places dogs are required to be on leash; however, the off-leash heel is a required part of obedience competition. It has some practical uses, too. If your Siberian is well trained, you can tell him to heel and walk him to your car or the mailbox without worrying about a leash. What happens if you are out on a walk and the leash or his collar breaks? It's happened before and will happen again. If your dog can heel by your side without a leash and collar, you won't need to panic.

Hook two leashes up to your dog's collar; his normal leash and a second, very lightweight leash. Do a watch me command with treats, then practice his heel work by having him walk nicely with you as you walk slow, fast, normal, and turn corners. Stop and have him sit while you praise him. Then reach down and unhook his regular leash and toss it to the ground in front of him. If he bounces up, thinking he's free, correct him, "I didn't release you!" and bring him back to the sit position. Hook his regular leash back up and repeat the exercise.

When he sits still for the leash to be tossed to the ground, continue by telling him to heel and then practice his heel work as you did with both leashes. Stop, have him sit, put the regular leash back on and repeat the whole thing again. Go back and forth between one leash and two so much that he won't remember what he has on. Repeat this over several training sessions. Remember to use the watch me command with treats to help keep his attention on you.

When he is to the point of behaving himself regardless of the leash or leashes, then take off the second leash. Fold his regular leash up and tuck it under his collar over his shoulder blades, so that it is on his back. Practice his heel work. If he makes a mistake or tries to take advantage, grab the leash on his back.

Expect (and demand) the same quality of work off leash that you expect when he's working on leash. Don't make excuses for mistakes off leash. Once your dog has mastered off-leash control, there is a

If you admire the fluffy, well groomed look of show dogs, you should consider using a hair dryer on your dog for after his bath. Start using it when he's a pup so he will learn to enjoy the experience. Photo courtesy of Metropolitan Vacuum Cleaner Co., Inc.

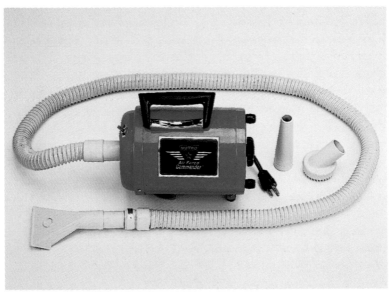

Photo by Isabelle Francais.

This little Husky is getting an early start on showing his enthusiasm for dog sports!

whole new world waiting for you both—dog sports!

DOG SPORTS

Have you discovered that you like training your Siberian Husky? A lot of Siberian owners start with puppy or basic training and discover that it is a lot more fun than they expected. For those who like training, there are a lot of dog sports that you and your Siberian can participate in. Some are just for fun, others are recreational or competitive, and a couple are in service for people.

Conformation Competition

The American Kennel Club (AKC) and the United Kennel Club (UKC) all award conformation championships to purebred dogs. The requirements vary between the registries, but basically the championship is earned when a purebred dog competes against other dogs of its breed and wins. When competing, the judge compares each dog to the standard for that breed and chooses the dog that most closely represents this written description.

In conformation your Siberian Husky is judged on how closely he conforms to the standard of the breed.

This is a very simplistic explanation; however, if you feel that your Siberian might be a good conformation candidate, write to either the American Kennel Club or the United Kennel Club and ask for information about competing in conformation. You will also want to do some reading on your breed and compare your dog to the written standard. You may also wish to attend a few dog shows in your area and watch the conformation competition to see if this is a sport you would be interested in.

Obedience Competition

Obedience competition is a team sport: the team consisting of you and your dog. There are set exercises that must be performed a certain way and both you and your dog are judged as to your ability to perform those exercises. Contrary to popular belief, many Siberian Huskies have done very well in obedience.

Both the American Kennel Club and the United Kennel Club sponsor obedience competition. There are also independent obedience tournaments—not associated with either the AKC or the UKC—held all over the country.

Again, you may wish to attend a local dog show and watch the obedience competition first. If this is something you would like to do, write to the AKC or UKC for a copy of their obedience competition rules and regulations. You will also need to find a dog trainer in your area experienced in obedience competition training to help you. There are also many books on the market that can help you prepare for competition.

Canine Good Citizen

The Canine Good Citizen program was introduced by the American Kennel Club in an effort to promote and reward responsible pet ownership.

Photo by Isabelle Francais.

Canine Good Citizens must be able to complete a series of exercises, including happily sitting for petting and social handling. This Husky looks like he's already passed the test.

During a Canine Good Citizen test, the dog and owner must complete a series of ten exercises, including sitting still for petting and grooming, walking nicely on a leash, sit, down, stay, and come. Upon completion of all ten exercises, the dog is awarded the title CGC.

For more information, contact the American Kennel Club or a dog trainer in your area.

Flyball

Is your Siberian, like so many others, absolutely tennis ball crazy? If so, then flyball is the sport for you. In flyball, dogs compete on a team. The dogs race over a course of hurdles, hit a machine that tosses a tennis ball, grab the ball, and race back over the hurdles. The team that finishes first, wins. Flyball has become so popular in some parts of the country that tournaments are held on a regular basis with numerous teams competing.

If your Siberian is tennis ball crazy, contact the North American Flyball Association for competition rules.

Temperament Test

The American Temperament Test Society was founded to provide breeders and trainers with a means of uniformly evaluating a dog's temperament. By using a standardized test, with each dog being tested in exactly the same manner, the test is used to compare and evaluate potential breeding stock, future working dogs, or simply as a way for dog owners to see how their dog might react in any given situation. This is very important for breeds such as the Siberian Husky, where personality and temperament problems have been known to occur.

For more information about the test and a schedule of tests in your area, write to the American Temperament Test Society.

Therapy Dogs

Although dog owners have always known how important our dogs are to us, researchers have now admitted that dogs are good medicine. Therapy dogs provide love, affection, warmth, closeness, and motivation to people who need it. Therapy dogs visit hospitals, nursing homes, day care centers, and hospices.

Scent Work

Does your Siberian use his nose to discover the world? Many do. Siberian Huskies have wonderful scenting abilities and have been used in many working situations because of

this talent. You can use your dog's scenting abilities, too, in tracking, for fun or for competition. Tracking competitions are offered by the American Kennel Club, with titles awarded for different levels of performance. Contact a dog trainer in your area for information about tracking classes or training. Write to the AKC for rules and regulations pertaining to tracking.

SNOW SPORTS

Siberians were bred to live and work in the snow; their coat is proof of that. If you live in snow country, you can teach your Siberian to pull the kids' sled, a skier, or if you want, a real dog sled. You can find help by contacting a local Siberian Husky club or a local dog trainer.

The Siberian Husky's coat allows them to live and work in colder climates.

Photo by Isabelle Francais.

Huskies thrive on regular exercise and love all activities, from jogging to playing to sledding, of course!

AGILITY

Agility is a fast growing and popular dog sport that combines a grand prix jumping event with an obstacle course. The dog must run through, jump over, and otherwise complete a series of obstacles in a set order. The dog is judged both by his manner of completing the course (safety is stressed) and how quickly he ran.

The American Kennel Club, United Kennel Club, and the United States Dog Agility Association sponsor agility competitions; write to them for rules and competition information.

Because of his background as a working dog, the Siberian Husky excels in sledding and snow sports.

siberian husky

Problem
PREVENTION
and Solving

Most of the behaviors that you might consider a problem—such as digging, barking, jumping on people, chewing, and so on—aren't problems to your Siberian Husky. Your dog digs because the dirt smells good, because the weather is hot and he wants to lie in some cooler dirt, or because you have gophers that he would like to play with. All of the things that you consider problems, your Siberian is doing for a reason. However, that doesn't mean that there is nothing you can do. Most problem behavior can be worked with and if it cannot be stopped entirely, it can be controlled or prevented.

WHAT CAN YOU DO?

Health Problems

Some experts feel that 20 percent of all behavior problems commonly seen are caused by health-related problems. A bladder infection can cause housetraining problems. Medications can cause behavior changes. Sometimes thyroid problems can cause a behavior problem, as can hyperactivity, hormone imbalances, and a variety of

Be sure that your Siberian Husky pup is provided with cool, clean water at all times—and that he can reach the bowl!

Photo by Isabelle Francais.

TRAINING

Training can play a big part in controlling problem behavior. A fair yet firm training program teaches your dog that you are in charge, that he is below you in the family dominance order, and should reinforce his concept of you as a kind, calm, caring leader. You can also use your training skills to teach your dog what is acceptable and what is not.

other health problems. If you have some concerns about your dog's physical health, make an appointment with your veterinarian.

Nutrition

Nutrition often plays a part in problem behavior. If your dog is not eating a good quality food, or if he isn't digesting his food properly, his body may be missing some vital nutrients. If your Siberian is chewing on rocks or wood, is eating the stucco off the side of your house, is grazing on the plants in your backyard, or is eating dirt, he may have a nutritional problem. Some dogs develop a type of hyperactivity when they eat a high calorie, high fat, high protein dog food. Other dogs have food allergies that might show up as behavior problems. If you have any questions about your dog's behavior in relation to food, or about the food you are feeding your dog, ask your veterinarian.

Play

Play is different from exercise, although exercise can

One of the fundamentals of good health throughout your dog's life is a sound, healthy diet. Photo courtesy of Nutro Products, Inc.

be play. Laughter is very much a part of play and that is what makes it so special. Researchers know that laughter is wonderful medicine—it makes you feel better—and because of that, it has a special place in your relationship with your dog. If training is sometimes difficult, and your dog is getting into trouble, make time to play with him. Play is a great stress reliever, both for you and for your dog, so make some time every day to laugh and play.

Sometimes dogs will intentionally get into trouble because they feel ignored. To some dogs, negative attention (corrections, yelling, and screaming) is better than no attention. By setting some time aside just for your Siberian, you can avoid some of these situations.

PREVENT PROBLEMS FROM HAPPENING

Because so many of the things we consider problems are not problems to your dog, you need to prevent them from happening as much as possible when you are not there to teach him. If your Siberian finds out how much fun it is to chew up your sofa cushion, throwing stuffing all over, you may have a difficult time stopping him. The same applies to the kitchen

Providing your Husky with safe toys specially made for dogs, like Nylafloss™, will keep boredom at bay and stop problem behavior before it starts.

Photo by Isabelle Francais.

Photo by Isabelle Francais.

The playful and active Siberian Husky needs regular activity and will enjoy a romp in the yard.

trash can that is full of scraps (treasures to your food-motivated Siberian!), the fruit trees in the backyard, and the children's toys. It's much easier to prevent a problem from happening than it is to break a bad habit. Preventing a problem from happening might require you to fence off the garden, build some new, higher shelves in the garage, or maybe even build your Siberian a new dog run.

DEALING WITH SPECIFIC PROBLEMS

Part of problem prevention also requires that you limit your dog's freedom. A young puppy or an untrained dog should never have unsupervised free

EXERCISE

Exercise is just as important for your Siberian as it is for you. It works the body, uses up excess energy, relieves stress, and clears the mind. How much exercise and what type depends upon your dog. A fast-paced walk might be enough exercise for a senior Siberian but a young healthy adult Siberian Husky will need a good long run or a fast paced game of ball. Maybe even a fast paced game of ball after a good run!

If your Siberian has some physical limitations or if you have any doubts about his exercise needs, talk to your veterinarian. When you start an exercise program, start gradually, especially if your dog has been a couch potato. Sore muscles are no fun.

Digging and Destroying the Garden

If your backyard looks like a military artillery range, you need to concentrate first on preventing these things from happening when you are not there to supervise your dog. If you come home eight to ten hours later and try to correct your dog for the hole he dug when you left for work, you are wasting your time; your correction is much too late. Instead of understanding that he is being corrected for digging, your Siberian is going to think he's being corrected for you coming home.

Siberians typically are not problem barkers, but they may bark or howl if bored and lonely.

Photo by Isabelle Francais.

run of the house; there is just too much he can get into. Instead, keep him in the room with you either by watching him or better yet, using baby gates across the doorways. If you can't keep him with you, then put him in his crate or outside in his yard.

HOUSEHOLD RULES

You may even need to institute some new household rules for you and other family members. Your dog can't raid the trash cans if you take the trash cans out before they are overflowing and put the trash cans away before you leave the house. Your Siberian will get into less trouble if everyone would close closet doors, pick up dirty laundry, and pick up their toys.

BUILD YOUR SIBERIAN A DOG RUN

Make the run big enough so that he can move around and trot back and forth. Make sure there is shade, unspillable water, and shelter from bad weather. When you leave him in the run, give him a toy or a treat and leave a radio on a soft, easy listening station in a nearby window.

When you're home, let your dog out for supervised runs in the backyard. When he starts to get into trouble, you can interrupt his actions and teach him what is acceptable and what is not.

The destructive dog also needs exercise, training, and play times every day to use up energy, stimulate his mind, and spend time with you. Most importantly, don't let your Siberian Husky landscape artist watch you garden; if you do, he will come to you later with all of those bulbs you planted earlier!

The Barker

Are your neighbors complaining because is serenading the neighborhood when you're at work? Siberians typically are not problem barkers but they may bark or howl if bored and lonely.

Start by teaching him to be quiet while you're at home. When your dog starts barking, tell him "Quiet!" When he stops barking, praise him, "Good boy to be quiet!"

When he understands what you want, go for a short walk outside, leaving your dog at home. Listen and when you hear him start barking, come back and correct him. After a few corrections, when your dog seems to have the idea, ask your neighbor to help you. Go outside, out front, and have your neighbor come out and talk. Maybe the kids can play and create a distraction. When

your dog barks, run back home as fast as you can and correct him again. Repeat as often as you need until he understands.

Some dogs will stop barking as you leave if you make leaving home very low-key and unexciting. A distraction also works well for many dogs. Take a small brown paper lunch bag and put a couple of treats in it, such as a dog biscuit, a piece of carrot, a slice of apple, and a small toy. Tape the top shut and rip a very tiny hole in the side of the bag. As you walk out the door or the gate, give this to your Siberian. He will be so busy trying to figure out what's inside that he won't pay attention to you leaving.

EXTRA HELP

Problem barkers may need extra help. There are anti-bark collars on the market, several of which are humane and effective. All are triggered by the dog's barking and administer a correction to the dog. Some collars make a high-pitched sound, one squirts a whiff of citronella, and others administer an electric shock. I do not recommend the shock treatment for most dogs; many will panic when corrected this way. However, the first two collars are quite effective with many dogs.

Dashing Through Doors and Gates

This is actually one of the easiest problems to correct. Teach your Siberian to sit and stay at all doors and gates and to hold that stay until you either give him permission to go through and release him after you have closed the door. By teaching him that doors and gates are boundaries that require permission, you will eliminate the problem.

Start with your dog on a leash and walk him up to the door. Have him sit, tell him to stay, and then with the leash firmly grasped in your hand, open the door wide and stand aside. If he dashes forward, correct him for breaking his stay, "No, stay!" Take him back where he started and do it again. If he continues to do it, give him a snap and release of the leash and collar as you correct him verbally. When he will hold the stay at this door, go to other doors and gates and teach the same lesson, the same way.

If your Siberian tries to sneak past you when he is not on the

A well-behaved Husky will stay at all doors and gates until given permission to go through— looks like these two fellas have learned their lessons well!

Photo by Isabelle Francais.

leash, block him with your leg or slam the door in his face as you give him a verbal correction.

If your dog does make it outside, don't chase him. If you chase him it becomes a game. Use your shaker to call him to you, "Sweetie, do you want a cookie? Come! Good boy!" When you do catch him or he comes back to you, don't correct him. If you do, he learns that coming back to you results in a correction. Instead, praise him for coming to you.

Jumping on People

Siberians are solid muscular dogs and can cause great damage if they jump on people. Your Siberian can't jump on you or other people if he's sitting; it's physically impossible to do both of those things at the same time. Since your dog jumps on people for attention, if you teach him to sit when you pet him you can eliminate the jumping.

When you come home from work and your dog is excited to see you, don't try to greet him with your arms full. Instead, greet him with empty hands. Then, when he tries to jump, grab him by the collar or the scruff of the neck and tell him to sit. When he sits, praise him,

Put your Siberian Husky's energy to work doing what the breed was made to do. This Husky gets a head start in a sledding competition.

"Good boy to sit!" and pet him. If he tries to jump up again, use your hands to put him back into the sitting position.

If your Siberian is really excited and it's very hard for him to control himself, once he's sitting, roll him over onto his back and give him a belly rub and a massage. This is still giving him the attention he needs but it is relaxing him at the same time.

You can also use the leash to teach your Siberian not to jump. When you are out for a walk and see your neighbor, don't let your neighbor pet your Siberian until you make him sit. If he starts to jump on your neighbor, use a snap and release of the leash and a verbal correction, "No jump! Sit." Use the same technique when guests come to your house; leash your dog before they come in.

The key to stopping your dog from jumping on people is to make sure that the bad behavior is not rewarded. If someone pets your Siberian Husky when he jumps up, the bad behavior is rewarded. When he learns that he gets all of the attention when he's sitting, then he will start sitting automatically for petting and when he does, praise him enthusiastically!

OTHER PROBLEMS

Many behavior problems can be solved, or at least controlled, by using similar techniques. Try to figure out why your Siberian is doing what he's doing (from his point of view, not yours), what you can do to prevent the problem from happening and what you can do to use your training skills to teach your dog. Remember that a correction alone will not solve the problem; you need to prevent the problem as much as possible and also teach your dog what he can do.

If you still have some unresolved problems or if your dog is showing aggressive tendencies, then contact your local dog trainer or behaviorist for expert help.

Remember that although training is hard work, it should fun and enjoyable for you and your Husky!

Photo by Isabelle Francais.

The time you invest in training your Husky will benefit the both of you for a lifetime. Good training will enable both of you to live life to its fullest.

s i b e r i a n h u s k y

Have Some FUN
With Your Training!

RETRIEVING

Most Siberian Huskies are not natural retrievers, unlike Labrador and Golden Retrievers who are willing and able to bring back anything that moves or is thrown. However, some Siberians will retrieve naturally, while others will chase after whatever is thrown but will not always bring it back. If your Siberian likes to retrieve, then all you need to do is fine tune the game so that he brings the item all the way back to you and gives it to you without playing tug of war. If he hesitates on the way back, simply call him to you. If he drops the item, send him back to it again, using encouragement to have him pick it up and bring it to you. Don't scold him or try to correct him; that will only serve to discourage him.

If your dog likes to take the thrown item and run with it, playing keep away, you have two options. You can stop the game and go inside, leaving him alone. This shows him that you will not chase him and the game will end when he tries to play keep away. Or you can have a long leash (a length of clothesline rope) on him when you start the game so that if he tries to play keep away, you can step on the rope, stop him, and use the rope to bring him back to you. If you need to use the rope, you still must praise him for coming back to you even if you made him do it. As has been said previously, the come must be positive.

HAVE FUN

Training has a tendency to be serious; after all, much of training is teaching your Siberian what his place in the family is and how to control himself. That can be serious stuff. However, training can also be fun. Games and trick training can challenge your training skills and your Siberian's ability to learn. However, once you have taught your dog a few tricks, you can have a great time showing off your dog's talent, amusing your friends and family, and just plain having fun with your dog.

Once your Siberian is retrieving reliably and bringing the toy back to you, there are

Photo by Isabelle Francais.

Introduce your Husky to safe, healthy Nylabone® toys at an early age and they will be his favorites for a lifetime!

Siberians can apply their talents to all kinds of activities. This Husky sizes up the bar jump.

unlimited games you can play. Tennis ball games are the game of choice for many dogs. To make it challenging, tennis balls can be throw short or far, or bounced off the side of the house. If your Siberian is really dedicated, throw several tennis balls and see how many he can pick up and carry at once!

THE NAME GAME

The name game is a great way to make your dog think. And don't doubt him for a minute, your dog can think and is capable of learning the names of many different items and people. Not only is this a great game for your Siberian, but it can come in handy around the house. Tell your dog to find your keys or your shoes. Send your Siberian after the remote control to the television, or to go find dad or mom. Plus, it's great fun to show off to your friends or guests!

Start with two items that are very different, perhaps a tennis ball and a bowl. Sit on the floor with your Siberian and those two items, and have some treats that he likes. Ask him, "Where's the ball?" and bounce the ball so that he tries to grab it or at least pays attention to it. When he touches it, tell him,

"Good boy to find the ball!" and give him a treat.

ONLY USE TOYS MADE FOR DOGS

Frisbee™ games are great fun. Throw a Nylabone® Frisbee™ and encourage your dog to chase it. When he jumps up after it, praise him enthusiastically. Go to a toy store and look in the aisle where Frisbees™ and balls are displayed. There are a variety of toys there that can make good retrieving dog toys—just keep your dog's safety in mind.

When he is responding to the ball, lay it on the floor next to the bowl and send him after it. Praise and reward him for getting it. Now set several different items out with the bowl and ball, and send him again. When he brings back the ball, praise and reward him. When he is doing that well, place one of his toys out there, too, and send him after it. If he goes for his other toy, take it away, with no comment, and send him after the ball again. This is a critical step in his learning process and you may need to repeat it several times.

When he will pick up his ball from among several different items, including other toys, then start hiding the ball. Make it simple to start, maybe just partially hidden under a magazine. As he gets better, start making it more challenging.

When you can hide the tennis ball and your dog can find it, start teaching him the names of other items, following the same process. You will find that the first three items will be the most difficult. Your dog needs to master the learning process and he needs to understand the concept you are trying to teach him. Once he understands that each of these

After a hard day at play, this Siberian needed a break!

Photo by Isabelle Francais.

things has a different sound, and that he needs to listen to you say those sounds, then he will start learning much faster.

HIDE AND SEEK

Hide and seek is a fun game, much like the hide and seek you played as a child, except that you or other family members will hide and your Siberian will find you. Your dog will be much better at finding people than you ever were, though, because he has such a sensitive nose and outstanding scenting abilities.

Start by teaching a family member's name (or your own) using the techniques you learned in the name game. When your dog can identify a family member, you can use that family member to hide. Give that family member a treat and have her show your dog that she has one. Hold your

Siberian as that family member goes and hides in a fairly easy location. Tell your dog, "Go find mom!" and let him go. If he starts to look around and sniff, just be quiet and let him work and think. If your dog starts to look flustered or confused, tell him again, "Go find mom!" and help him find her. When he goes to mom, praise him enthusiastically and let mom give your dog the treat.

THE COME GAME

In this game, two family members will stand or sit across the room or yard from each other. Each will have some treats for your Siberian. Taking turns, each will call your dog to come and when he does, praise and reward him. This is a very simple game but gives you a chance to practice the come command and makes it fun at the same time. Plus, everyone in the family can practice it, giving even the kids a chance to "train" your dog.

Pleased to meet you! The fun-loving Husky will happily perform for his master.

Photo by Isabelle Francais.

As your dog gets better at this game, you can start making it more challenging. Have family members hide in more difficult places or slightly farther away from your Siberian. They can also run around a little before finding a hiding place, so that there is a more challenging trail. As your Siberian gets better, you can also cover his eyes so that he can't see the family member go hide.

When your dog has learned the names of different family members and knows how to find them, you can use this skill around the house. Send your Siberian out to the yard to get the kids when it's dinnertime. Or have him take the TV remote control to dad when he asks for it. Hide and seek is a lot of fun, is challenging for your dog, and uses his natural scenting abilities.

WAVE

When he is shaking hands reliably, tell him "Shake. Wave!" and instead of shaking his paw, just lightly touch your hand under his paw and move your hand away so that he continues to reach for your hand. As he reaches for your hand, tell him, "Good to wave!" With the wave, you want him to lift his paw higher than in the shake and to move it up and down so that he looks like he is waving.

TREAT ON NOSE

Have your Siberian sit and stay. Hold his chin with one hand as you place a treat on the top of his nose. Tell him "Stay!" After a few seconds, tell him,

"Okay!" and let him toss the treat and catch it. Gradually increase the time you want him to wait before you release him and enthusiastically praise him when he catches the treat in mid-air.

SHAKE HANDS

Shaking hands is a very easy trick to teach your dog. Have your Siberian sit in front of you and ask him to "Shake" as you reach behind one front paw and tickle his leg in the hollow just behind his paw. When he lifts his paw to escape the tickle, shake his paw as you tell him, "Good to shake!" and give him a treat. When he starts to lift his paw on his own, stop tickling.

ROLL OVER

Have your Siberian lie down. With a treat in one

It is important to keep in mind that your puppy wants to please you and with patience will learn what you have to teach him.

Photo by Isabelle Francais.

hand, circle your Siberian's head with the treat in the direction you want him to roll, while you tell him, "Roll over!" At first, you may need to physically help him roll. Praise him when he does roll over, even if you need to help him. Enthusiastically praise him when he does it on his own.

Once he can roll over by himself, you can ask him to do it more than once. Have him roll over two or three times. Teach him a command for each, "Three roll overs!" or "Two roll overs!" Impress your friends that your dog knows how to count!

Remember all the fun you had running and playing as a child? Your Siberian Husky will love it too—but be careful; his athletic prowess will make keeping up quite a challenge!

AND THERE'S MORE!
Trick training is limited only to what you want to teach your dog. Teach him to crawl, to play dead, or to sit up and beg. Teach him to dance. What would you (and your dog!) enjoy?

Whether puppy or adult, you can teach any dog new tricks! Apply yourself to training with dedication and love and you will see your dog's real potential.

Photo by Isabelle Francais.

This is a Siberian Husky with promise. With proper training any dog has the potential to become a valued and welcomed member of your family.

siberian husky

SUGGESTED READING

Books By T.F.H. Publications

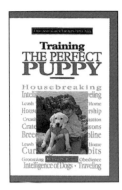

JG-109
Training The Perfect Puppy
By Andrew DePrisco
160 pages, over 200 color photos

TS-205
Successful Dog Training
By Michael Kamer, OSB
160 pages, over 150 color photos

TS-258
Training Your Dog for Sports and
Other Activities
By Charlotte Schwartz
160 pages, 170 full-color photos

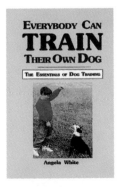

TW-113
Everybody Can Train
Their Own Dog
By Angela White
256 pages, 200 color photos

WW-009
Housebreaking and Training Puppies
By J.R. Gardner
64 pages, 79 full-color photos

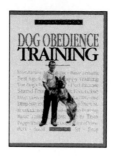

WW-025
Dog Obedience Training
By Ross Allan
64 pages, over 100 full-color photos

TS-252
Dog Behavior and Training
By Lowell Ackerman, DVM
288 pages, over 170 full-color photos

KW-022
Basic Dog Training
By Miller Watson
96 pages, over 100 full-color photos

JG-117
Dog Training
By Dorman Pantfoeder
160 pages, over 100 full-color photos

TS-283
Training Problem Dogs
By Dr. Louis Vine
256 pages, 50 drawings

JG-127
A New Owner's Guide to Siberian Huskies
By Kathleen Kanzler
160 pgs, 150 full-color photos

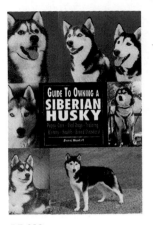

RE-310
Guide to Owning a Siberian Husky
By Alexi Montoff
64 pgs, 50 full-color photos

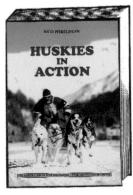

TS-234
Huskies in Action
By Rico Pfirststinger
140 pgs, 120 full-color photos

TS-148
The Siberian Husky
By Joan McDonald Brearly
512 pgs, 600 full-color photos